P9-DWI-183

Who Is
Ralph Lauren?

by Jane O'Connor

illustrated by Stephen Marchesi

Penguin Workshop
An Imprint of Penguin Random House

For Stephanie Spinner, a classic dresser—JOC

For Bernadette, valued friendships endure—SM

PENGUIN WORKSHOP
Penguin Young Readers Group
An Imprint of Penguin Random House LLC

If you purchased this book without a cover, you should be aware that this book is stolen property. It was reported as "unsold and destroyed" to the publisher, and neither the author nor the publisher has received any payment for this "stripped book."

Penguin supports copyright. Copyright fuels creativity, encourages diverse voices, promotes free speech, and creates a vibrant culture. Thank you for buying an authorized edition of this book and for complying with copyright laws by not reproducing, scanning, or distributing any part of it in any form without permission. You are supporting writers and allowing Penguin to continue to publish books for every reader.

Copyright © 2017 by Penguin Random House LLC. All rights reserved. Published by Penguin Workshop, an imprint of Penguin Random House LLC, 345 Hudson Street, New York, New York 10014. PENGUIN and PENGUIN WORKSHOP are trademarks of Penguin Books Ltd. WHO HQ & Design is a registered trademark of Penguin Random House LLC. Printed in the USA.

Library of Congress Cataloging-in-Publication Data is available.

ISBN 9781524784027 (paperback)   10 9 8 7 6 5 4 3 2 1
ISBN 9781524784034 (library binding)   10 9 8 7 6 5 4 3 2 1

Contents

Who Is Ralph Lauren?

Growing up in the 1950s, Ralph loved going to the movies. For him, it was like entering another world, one that was completely different from the Bronx neighborhood in New York City where he lived.

When they were old enough, Ralph and his friends would go by themselves to the Paradise Theatre. It seemed like a palace, with seats for four thousand people, marble columns, statues everywhere, a grand staircase, and even a fountain with goldfish swimming in it.

The movies were often action-packed war stories, or Westerns with famous stars like John Wayne. For Ralph, seeing a movie wasn't just about watching an exciting story unfold on a big screen. He could actually picture himself *in* the movie.

He *was* John Wayne, riding off to catch the bad guys, wearing a cowboy hat, chaps, and dust-covered boots.

Although Ralph's family wasn't poor, his parents didn't have a lot of money to buy their kids new clothes. The youngest of four children, Ralph often wore hand-me-downs from his older brother Jerry. Jerry was Ralph's idol and best friend. So Ralph didn't mind. He felt comfortable in clothes that already had been broken in for him. It made him feel cool to put on something like an old team jacket of Jerry's.

Of course, Ralph also wanted to choose his own clothes. And by the time he was a teenager, he already had a clear sense of his own style.

He didn't dress like his friends. Most of them wore white T-shirts and jeans. They wanted to look like Elvis Presley, who was the hottest rock star of the 1950s. Not Ralph. He'd save up for a V-necked tennis sweater or a pair of tweed shorts. He looked like he belonged on the campus of Harvard or Yale rather than in the school yard.

Did other kids think this was weird?

No. In fact, just the opposite. They thought Ralph was cool.

As he grew older, Ralph began to think that a lot of other guys might want to dress the way he did. So in his late twenties, he began designing ties. They were wider and cooler than the drab ties men wore in the mid-1960s. Ralph had the ties made by hand. Then he went around with a box of ties, trying to get stores to sell them.

Have you heard of Ralph Lauren (say: LOR-en)? Even if you don't recognize his name, certainly you know his company. The logo is a polo player

on horseback, holding a
raised mallet. Ralph started
with ties, but fifty years
later, his company designs
much more than clothes for
men, women, and children.
There are Ralph Lauren
sheets and towels, furniture,
and fragrances. You can
buy Ralph Lauren watches,
sunglasses, handbags, underwear, suitcases,
chocolate bars, and coffee. There is even a line of
Ralph Lauren house paint, which offers thousands
of colors, including fifty-one shades of white.

What do all these different things have in
common?

They share Ralph Lauren's unique sense of
taste *and style*.

Everything he designs is something he would
want to own himself.

Through hard work, lots of imagination, and a strong belief in himself, Ralph Lauren has created a multibillion-dollar fashion empire. His story is a very American story. It stands as proof that someone can start out with little, follow a dream, and end up doing something amazing with their life.

CHAPTER 1
A Boy from the Bronx

Ralph was born on October 14, 1939, in the Bronx, one of New York City's five boroughs. His family's last name was Lifshitz. (Like many children of immigrants with hard-to-pronounce last names, Ralph and his brother Jerry later changed theirs—in this case from Lifshitz to Lauren.)

Ralph's parents, Frieda and Frank, had each come to the United States from Russia. They were both Jewish. In Russia in the early 1900s, Jewish people were the frequent targets of *pogroms*—violent attacks supported by the government.

As a child, Ralph watched his parents studying for the test to become citizens. That was very important. In the United States, Frieda and Frank

Coming to America

From 1880 to the early 1920s, a great wave of immigrants came to the United States—a total of twenty-three million people. Ralph's parents were among them. His father, Frank, arrived in 1920; his mother, Frieda, came in 1921. Most immigrants at that time had been born in eastern Europe. Many were Jewish people who settled in New York City in

neighborhoods like the one Ralph Lauren grew up in. Newly arrived immigrants hoped for better lives than the ones they had left behind. For them, a better life meant more than finding a decent job. They now were free to follow their religious beliefs. This is the same reason the Pilgrims came to America in the 1600s.

had found a better future where they could raise a family safely and freely. First came their daughter, Thelma, born in 1929, followed by three sons: Lenny, Jerry, and the baby, Ralph.

The family lived in a brick building across from a park. Their two-bedroom apartment was tight quarters for six people—Thelma had to sleep on a pullout sofa. But it was a lively, happy home where there was almost always the smell of something good cooking.

Ralph was a playful, imaginative kid. When he pretended to be Superman, he didn't just pin on a towel for a cape. Oh no. He'd put on glasses and wear Superman pj's under his clothes so he could "transform" himself from wimpy Clark Kent into the Man of Steel.

All four of the Lifshitz siblings were artistic. (Ralph has always insisted that he was the least talented and never very good at drawing.) Whatever their talent, it came from their father.

A friendly, kindhearted man, Frank was a painter. Sometimes he was hired to create murals—scenes painted directly on walls or ceilings—in the lobbies of office buildings in Manhattan.

Those were the jobs he found most rewarding. But to earn enough money to support his family, he often painted apartments. Even with those jobs, Frank was creative. He could paint a wall to look like it was made of marble or wood.

Sometimes Ralph would help his father, carrying supplies and painting a little himself. He learned the importance of taking pride in one's work. The importance of always doing one's best.

Small and pretty, Frieda stayed home caring for the children. She took great pride in her tight-knit family. Very different in nature from Frank, Frieda was a practical woman for whom religion was very important. As she had done with his brothers, Frieda sent Ralph to a local yeshiva, a school that focused on Jewish studies. If his mother had had her way, Ralph would have become a rabbi. But that didn't interest Ralph at all. Much later in his life, in a magazine article, Ralph remembered how his mother "would light the Sabbath candles on Friday night." He said she "gave us a sense of love in family, a sense of accomplishment, a sense of religion, and a sense of warmth."

When he wasn't inside a classroom or a movie theater, he was outside playing baseball and basketball. Ralph was sports-crazy! Joe DiMaggio and Mickey Mantle of the New York Yankees were his heroes. Although not as tall as his friends,

Ralph was a good athlete. He had a great hook shot on the basketball court and plenty of drive. He gave every game his best.

In winter, everyone went sledding down the steep hill in the nearby park. One time, when Ralph was about twelve, he and a bunch of friends got in a snowball fight with some other boys they hardly knew. It started out as fun but then turned kind of nasty.

Soon the other boys started chanting, "We want Ralph! We want Ralph!"

Ralph could have run away. But instead he got mad. He said, "You want me? Then here I come!"

Ralph jumped on his sled and bombed down the hill, heading straight toward them. The boys all scattered. They were the ones who ran away.

Later on, as a much older man, he recalled this as a "victorious moment." Ralph was proud that he stood up for himself.

The school yard was right across the street from Ralph's home. The iron fence surrounding it was called the Rail. After classes were over and on weekends, everybody would hang out at the Rail, Ralph included. Although soft-spoken, Ralph always had a lot of friends. What made him stand out from the crowd at the Rail were his clothes.

By the time Ralph entered DeWitt Clinton High School, he had definite ideas about the way to dress. He wore button-down shirts, khaki pants, and wool crewneck sweaters. Today it would be called a preppy look. Back then it was known as traditional. Ralph wore the clothes well, carrying himself with confidence. Girls thought he looked great. And of course, it didn't hurt that Ralph had a great smile and blue eyes.

Stickball

If Ralph and his friends couldn't get to a baseball field, they could always play stickball in the street outside. Stickball is a lot like baseball, but with a broom handle used for a bat, and a rubber ball instead of a baseball. Sometimes a manhole cover will serve as home base. Up through the 1970s, the game was very popular among city kids in New York and Philadelphia. Today, in parts of the Bronx and in cities across the country, stickball is still played.

Ralph's traditional clothes weren't hand-me-downs from Jerry. And they were also more expensive than any clothes Ralph's mother would have bought for the boys. To pay for them, Ralph started working part-time. In high school, he became a stock boy at a department store. (A stock boy keeps track of clothes that are returned so they can be put back on racks and resold.)

Ralph also took a summer job at Camp
Roosevelt in upstate New York. This was the
first time Ralph was away from his close-knit
community of family and friends. The campers
and many of the counselors came from families
that were much more well-off than Ralph's.

At first he felt out of place, but that soon changed. He loved the three summers he spent at Roosevelt. He became head counselor and was chosen as the "general" of one of the two teams during color war, an all-important week of games

and sports contests. Being a general was the greatest honor at Roosevelt. It meant Ralph was a leader.

Even sixty years later, Ralph considers his camp days important. His sense of self-worth grew. He began to see something special in himself.

CHAPTER 2
Starting Out

In the yearbook at DeWitt Clinton High School, underneath the photo of every student was written their dream for the future. For many, that meant becoming a doctor or lawyer. Not Ralph. He wrote that he wanted to be a millionaire. As he grew older, Ralph regretted putting that down because it sounded as if he only cared about money. That wasn't so. For Ralph as a kid, becoming a millionaire meant doing something great with your life.

RALPH LIFSHITZ

C.C.N.Y.

Lunch Room Squad, "Clinton News," Dean's Office Squad, Health Ed. Squad

Millionaire

The problem was, he had no idea how to do that. He certainly never imagined becoming a fashion designer. In fact, in high school, he didn't have a clue what being a fashion designer even meant. After graduating from DeWitt Clinton in 1957 with no clear career path, Ralph enrolled at City College of New York. He took business classes there, but they didn't provide him with a clearer sense of direction, either. So after two years he dropped out, served in the United States Army, and then found a job at Brooks Brothers.

There, Ralph could learn about the men's clothing business.

Located on Madison Avenue and Forty-Fourth Street in Manhattan, Brooks Brothers had been in business since 1818. It sold the kind of preppy sports clothes seen on boys at Harvard, Yale, and Princeton, as well as the suits, blazers, and ties that their fathers wore. The store had a long and rich history. For Ralph, quite simply, it was the real deal.

As a salesman, Ralph soaked up the atmosphere at Brooks Brothers. He was eager to please customers, and he developed an even sharper eye for what did—and did not—look good on men. Like his father, he threw himself into his work. He gave his job 100 percent effort.

About two and a half years later, a better job came Ralph's way. He didn't know it then, but he was about to discover his life's work. It began with something very simple.

Men's neckties.

CHAPTER 3
Ricky

Nineteen sixty-four was a very important year for Ralph. Besides starting a new job at A. Rivetz & Co., a company that made ties, he met a beautiful young woman named Ricky Ann Low-Beer.

From the time he started hanging out at the Rail, Ralph had always been popular with girls. But he had never dated anyone seriously—not until Ricky. She was five years younger than Ralph, going to Hunter College, and working part-time in an eye doctor's office.

Ralph came in for an eye exam one day, saw Ricky, and asked her out. When he came to pick her up, Ralph arrived dressed in a suit. That impressed Ricky and her parents.

Ricky was very shy—except on the dance floor. She was amazing! She had supreme confidence. Seeing her dance was part of what made Ralph fall in love and propose to her. She didn't say yes. Not right away. But then six months later, on December 20, 1964, Ralph and Ricky were married.

To put it simply, they were right for each other. Small, slim, with long blond hair and ice-blue eyes, Ricky was smart, cheerful, and down-to-earth. Like Ralph, Ricky was Jewish and had grown up in New York City. And like Ralph, she, too, had parents who had emigrated from Europe to America. The Low-Beers shared the same basic values as Ralph's parents. Family and hard work were what mattered. Beyond that, Ricky was dazzled by Ralph; he was exciting and had a lot of self-confidence. He wanted to do something big with his life. She had faith that he would.

While Ricky was finishing college, Ralph was working hard for Rivetz, the tie company. They made ties for Brooks Brothers, Bloomingdale's, and other high-priced department stores. The ties were the typical-looking ones worn by businessmen. They came in dark colors and were narrow—about three inches across. From year to year, patterns never changed much.

The other Rivetz salesmen were all a lot older than Ralph and wore baggy business suits, along with the ties they sold. They didn't know what to make of twenty-five-year-old Ralph. It wasn't just how young he was, it was the way he dressed. Sometimes he wore corduroy riding  pants and a beat-up leather bomber jacket to see customers. When he wore suits, they were like the ones men in Europe wore. More fitted and made of finer material. As for the car he drove, it wasn't a practical four-door sedan.

It was a two-seater convertible English sports car. Who did Ralph think he was? A movie star?

The head of Rivetz—Abe—got a kick out of Ralph. Ralph was charming and full of energy, and Abe saw something special in him. Ralph understood that fashion for men was changing. He wanted to design the kind of ties he liked— ones that were wider, more colorful, and made of unique fabrics. But that wasn't going to happen at Rivetz. After Abe died, an executive said, "Ralph, you're like a diamond but with rough edges. The world isn't ready for Ralph Lauren."

Actually, the world *was* ready for Ralph Lauren. A. Rivetz & Co. just wasn't. So Ralph switched jobs and went to Beau Brummell, another tie manufacturer. Again, Ralph asked to design a line of ties. This time the answer was yes, and he was given a chance to start his own division.

In April of 1967, Ralph showed up at a tiny, windowless office in the Empire State Building.

All he had was a single drawer to work out of!

From the start, Ralph had an eye for choosing unusual fabrics that appealed to him. Once, he even saw a tablecloth that he was sure could be turned into terrific-looking ties. He didn't know how to cut cloth or sew. No matter. He found a skilled tailor to do that. Ricky and her mother helped sew labels onto the ties at the Laurens' kitchen table.

Ralph named his line of ties Polo.

Polo

Why did Ralph Lauren call his company Polo?

Polo captures the glamorous and sporty image that Ralph wanted for his company. Often called "the sport of kings," polo is played on horseback. On a grassy field, two teams of four players go against each other, trying to score by whacking a ball (usually made of wood) into the opposing team's goal. Matches last about ninety minutes and are divided into periods called chukkers.

Polo is fast and dangerous. Once hit, a ball may travel at a speed of up to 110 miles per hour. The sport originated in central Asia over a thousand years ago but became popular in Great Britain and certain parts of the United States in the late 1800s. Prince William and Prince Harry of England are both enthusiastic polo players.

Soon Ralph was visiting different shops with a box of his ties. He wanted to change the world of men's fashion . . . and ties were just the beginning.

CHAPTER 4
Like No Other Store in the World

Most people like a bargain. So it might be reasonable to think that in the early days, Ralph sold his ties to stores at a lower price than the ties from Rivetz and other companies. After all, Ralph was an unknown, whereas his competitors had been selling ties to department stores like Brooks Brothers for decades. If Ralph's ties were less expensive, then maybe stores would take a chance and buy his.

But in fact, Ralph did just the opposite. In the late 1960s, a man's tie usually sold for $3.50. Polo ties cost between $7.50 and $15. That was unheard of, unthinkable! But this made sense because Ralph's ties were much wider, handmade, and used costly fabrics.

Why did Ralph want his new, wider ties to be so expensive? He wanted customers to understand that when they bought a Polo tie, they were getting the best. A luxury. So of course the tie would cost more money. If a bargain was what people were looking for, Polo wasn't for them.

Right from the beginning, Ralph Lauren had very strong ideas about Polo's image. Just like the sport, it reflected an upper-class world, the kind of world that Ralph dreamed of living in one day.

The kind of world pictured in glamorous romantic comedies starring Cary Grant or Fred Astaire. They were just the sort of men to wear a Polo tie.

And Bloomingdale's was just the store where Ralph wanted his ties to be sold. In the 1960s and 1970s, the department store on Fifty-Ninth Street and Lexington Avenue carried the latest in everything.

Cary Grant

Fred Astaire

Billing itself as "a store like no other," it became a New York City landmark. Tourists felt they had to return home with something in a Bloomie's shopping bag. Even the queen of England paid a visit.

Ralph took his bag of three-and-a-half-inch-wide ties to the buyer at Bloomingdale's. There were plaids, paisleys, and stripes in all kinds of fabrics never used before to make ties.

The buyer looked them over and—lo and behold!—he wanted the store to buy the ties so they could sell them to their customers. But there was a hitch. Ralph remembers that the buyer told him, "Ralph, I like the patterns—but you gotta make [the ties] a quarter of an inch narrower. And I want you to take your name off." Instead of Ralph's Polo label, the Bloomingdale's label would be sewn on the ties.

Store-Bought Clothes

Before the middle of the 1800s, most people in the United States lived on farms and made their own clothes. That changed with the invention of the sewing machine in 1846. It led to businesses springing up to manufacture and sell clothes. In time, every city had a department store where customers could buy an entire wardrobe.

New York City became the center of clothes-making in the United States. Part of the reason was

that millions of immigrants from Germany and central Europe came to New York City in the late 1800s. Many of the women had sewing skills. Many men had been tailors. By 1900, clothes-manufacturing was the top industry in New York City. However, a century later, only a fraction of the clothing designed there was produced in the United States. That is because it cost much less to have clothes manufactured in countries such as Mexico, China, and India.

Perhaps that doesn't sound like a lot to ask. But to Ralph, it was. He told the buyer that even though he was "dying to sell to Bloomingdale's," he couldn't take his own label off. The ties were designed by him, not by anyone at Bloomingdale's; the ties should have his name on them. Also, he wouldn't make the ties even a quarter inch narrower. He thought the ties were perfect as they were.

So . . . what happened next?

Bloomingdale's didn't take Ralph's ties.

Friends thought he was crazy. Who turns down Bloomingdale's? What was a quarter inch? Who would notice other than Ralph?

But that was the point. Ralph would notice. Making a sale—even to Bloomingdale's—wasn't as important as staying true to himself. And that meant making something exactly the way he thought was best. Ralph also trusted that there were men out there with the same sense of style that he had. So he didn't back down and continued carrying his box of ties to stores in New York and other cities. Many stores sold them, and style-conscious men bought them. They didn't care about the high price tag. Cash registers kept ringing up sales. Within half a year, Ralph sold a quarter of a million dollars' worth of his ties.

So . . . what happened next?

The Late Sixties

The 1960s were known as a time of political protest. They were also known as a time when young people changed the way they dressed. It was a new age, when men as well as women became style-conscious.

The big fashion changes for men started in England with the "Carnaby Street" look. Carnaby Street was the street in London where shops sold purple velvet suits for young men, five-inch-wide ties, and pointy-toed shoes in wild colors and with higher heels. Clothes became more like costumes. Probably the best known example of this new look was the Beatles.

Bloomingdale's came back to Ralph. Now that he was gaining popularity, the store would sell Ralph's ties—with his label on them. There was no longer any talk of making them narrower, because by this time, Bloomingdale's understood that Ralph Lauren was a hot property.

CHAPTER 5
Not Just Ties Anymore

Clearly, men would want more fashionable shirts and suits to wear with all the Polo ties they were buying. Ralph wanted to design those, too— an entire line of clothes for men. They would be the kind of suits Ralph liked to wear—stylishly cut and made of the best fabrics, with attention to detail, down to the kind of buttons on them and how the pockets were sewn. But making shirts and suits—especially very high-quality ones—

was not only much more complicated than making ties. It was also more expensive.

Where was Ralph Lauren going to get the money to do this?

Norman Hilton ran a family-owned factory in New Jersey that made suits sold in fine department stores. He was looking for someone to design shirts and ties for his suits. He had heard about Ralph Lauren and met with him, asking, "Would you like to work for me?"

But Ralph told Norman Hilton, "I don't want to work for anybody." He wanted to start his own company.

Hilton took Ralph at his word. But as with the Bloomingdale's tie buyer, Hilton came back not long after with another offer. He'd loan Ralph enough money—about $50,000—to start a company.

This was the birth of Polo menswear. First came dress shirts, quickly followed by tailored

jackets, trousers, coats, and suits. Ralph designed
everything. Ralph followed his own sense of taste.
He was now able to design the clothes he would
want to wear himself.

Peter Strom

Ralph was able to leave Beau Brummell and
keep the name Polo for his new company. But he
could no longer be a one-man show. He needed
help. Peter Strom, who had worked for Hilton,
joined Ralph's new company. He saw to it that the
clothes were manufactured properly and reached
stores on time.

Ralph also hired a young woman named Buffy Birrittella. She would help with design and advertising. A former fashion reporter, she admired Ralph's sense of style and his refusal to ever lower his standards. She was excited about where Ralph was heading. She wanted to be part of it. More than forty-five years later, Buffy is still making her mark at Polo. She and Ralph have worked together so closely that other people say it almost seems as if Buffy can read his mind.

Jerry Lauren

Ralph also turned to Jerry Lauren, who understood Ralph in a way that no one but a brother could. Jerry would run all of men's design. He, too, is still with the company.

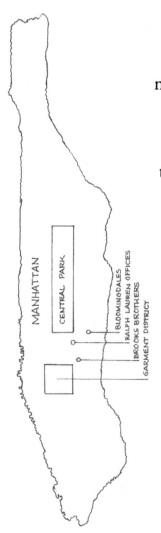

MANHATTAN

CENTRAL PARK

BLOOMINGDALES
RALPH LAUREN OFFICES
BROOKS BROTHERS
GARMENT DISTRICT

Although Norman Hilton was his partner, Ralph chose not to work from Hilton's New York City offices. They were in a neighborhood known as the Garment District, because so many clothing companies had showrooms and offices there. Ralph wanted to keep his independence, so he found offices in a building in Midtown Manhattan—just west of Fifth Avenue on Fifty-Fifth Street. (After twenty-five years, company headquarters moved to its present location nearby, on Fifty-Ninth Street and Madison Avenue.)

Ralph Lauren's first line of men's clothes came out in 1968. The clothes were an instant hit. They were classically styled but with a special sense of flair. Bloomingdale's gave Ralph his own boutique, almost like a little store within the store, where his clothes—and only his—would be sold. This had never happened before. Until then, ties, shirts, and suits from many different designers had been displayed by categories—shirts were together, ties were together, and so on.

Ralph Lauren Stores

Besides Ralph Lauren shops in large department stores, there are hundreds of Ralph Lauren stores that sell only his clothes. They are found all across the United States and also in major cities the world over, including Paris, France; Tokyo, Japan; Hong Kong, China; and Cairo, Egypt.

The flagship (most important) Ralph Lauren store is on Madison Avenue in New York City. Ralph took over a huge mansion that looked like it belonged in the English countryside, not on the corner of a busy city street. It was very run-down, but Ralph restored the building to its former grandeur—with oak floors, Persian rugs, crystal chandeliers, and marble fireplaces. There are four floors displaying Ralph Lauren clothes and products. However, customers don't come to the store just to shop. They are coming for an experience. Ralph has created a store that functions like a giant set where the customers become the stars of the movie as soon as they put on Ralph Lauren clothes.

Not only was Ralph designing the clothes, he also designed the space they were sold in. The Ralph Lauren boutique at Bloomingdale's had wood-paneled walls, leather armchairs, and old prints. Customers would say that they felt as if they had stepped inside an exclusive men's club.

That was just the reaction Ralph wanted. He wasn't merely designing clothes; he was offering the world where people wearing Ralph Lauren clothes belonged.

CHAPTER 6
Men's Clothes for Women?

Ralph was a success. He and Ricky moved into a larger and nicer apartment in Manhattan. They started a family. Their first son, Andrew, was born in 1969. David followed two years later, and in 1974, Dylan (a baby girl) arrived on the scene.

Ralph had been a playful kid; now he could have fun being a playful dad. There were fierce Lauren family Ping-Pong games after dinner and all kinds of silly contests—even one for who could make the best milk shake.

As Ralph grew more famous, he and Ricky could have been out at fancy parties every night. Instead, they preferred staying home, watching a movie, or inviting grandparents over on Sundays.

When they had time, Ralph and Ricky loved to window shop and discuss clothes. Ricky always had trouble finding what she wanted—for example, she liked shirts cut like a man's, and men's sports jackets small enough to fit her.

This gave Ralph an idea. Why not create a fashion line for women, and design the kinds of clothes Ricky wanted to wear? In 1971, he began by making crisp, tailored shirts in fine cotton. They had the look and quality of a man's dress shirt but were fitted to a woman's body. The logo of the inch-tall polo player with his mallet raised was stitched on the shirt cuff.

The shirts were a sensation; women had to have them. They were a status symbol. The polo player became proof of a woman's style and fashion sense.

Just as with menswear, Ralph quickly expanded his line for women. It offered all the kinds of clothes that Ricky looked great in, like tweed jackets and pleated trousers. To Ralph, women looked beautiful in masculine clothes.

Over the years, Ricky

Polo Shirts

Before Ralph Lauren came on the scene, short-sleeved cotton-knit sports shirts were popular with both men and women. They were called tennis shirts or golf shirts or polo shirts. Ralph decided to make better ones. They came in softer cotton and many more colors, and had the polo player logo on the chest. They were an instant hit and made the little polo player as widely known a symbol as the Nike swoosh, the McDonald's arched *M*, and Apple's partially eaten apple!

has continued to inspire
many of Ralph's designs.
His famous handbag—
the Ricky—is named
for her.

Soon, Ralph was designing collections of
women's clothes, one line for spring and one for
fall. Each line featured about fifty outfits that
included dresses, skirts, evening gowns, shoes,
and accessories. It was presented at a fashion show
to buyers and reporters, as well as celebrities.

For a fashion designer, every collection has to present fresh, original outfits. So that means coming up with thousands of ideas every year. Ralph Lauren couldn't limit himself strictly to a man's look in clothing for women. Nor did he want to. Designing women's clothes let loose all of Ralph's creative powers.

Each of Ralph's collections was almost always built around a theme—like the Old West, Ivy League colleges, the military, or life in an English manor. Ralph's ideas came from whatever he saw in life that he loved.

Sometimes the themes came from places he had never been. He wondered, what would a woman wear on a safari in Africa? What would she see? Where would she sleep? He pictured it all as if he were making a mini-movie.

Sometimes a line of clothes was inspired by something as unlikely as a car. Ralph was the  proud owner of a sleek black Porsche sports car. So he decided to design clothes—all in black—to go with it.

Other collections were based on places that he had visited and that made a deep impression on him. Most especially places in the United States. For example, in 1980, the Lauren family visited the Southwest for the first time. Ralph and Ricky

fell in love with the land—the open spaces, the earthy tones of the desert, the sharp brilliance of the sky, and the beauty of Native American art. Ralph expressed all of this in one of his most successful lines of women's clothes. He called it the Santa Fe collection.

Ralph had never been to design school or learned to sketch. So for him, the process of creating clothes was different from that of many other designers. Once he chose a theme, ideas would come to him for different dresses and outfits. Then Ralph would describe what he wanted to a sketcher. Ralph was like a writer telling a story or picturing a movie. Sketch artists

who worked with Ralph for a long time came to know and understand Ralph. They could take what he was describing and transfer it into a drawing. They'd keep sketching until what was on paper matched what was in Ralph's imagination.

From there, a rough sample of the outfit could be made for a "fit model" to try on. From seeing a real version of his idea, Ralph would make changes.

Also, Ralph might end up not liking the original fabric he'd picked once he saw it as an actual piece of clothing. So the sample would be made up in other fabrics and colors. Ralph always felt that no matter how good something ended up, it could always be better. This was sometimes hard for people working with him because he was such a perfectionist. No detail was ever too small to discuss, change, and then change again many times.

Once a collection was designed, how it was presented to the public was as important to Ralph as the clothes themselves. One way to reach customers is through ads in magazines, and commercials on TV and online.

Ralph Lauren completely changed the way men's and women's fashion is advertised. Because he was always telling a story through his clothes, he needed to do more in a magazine ad than simply show a photograph of a model wearing a shirt or a pair of pants that he had designed. Instead, he created pages and pages of models in his clothes appearing in the actual setting— for instance, models in safari outfits would be shown exploring the wild. By doing this, Ralph was explaining to customers what had inspired the collection. (Once, he ran a magazine ad that didn't show any clothes at all—just a barn!)

For TV, his commercials were like minute-
long movies that again showcased the life of the
man or woman in his fashions, whether they were
in ski clothes on mountain slopes or partygoers at
a country estate.

Fashion shows have always been another way to create excitement around a collection. That is when stores send their buyers to decide what outfits will be sold. Fashion reporters come to write reviews of the collection for magazines and newspapers.

The shows themselves are always lavish and splashy. The one for Ralph's Santa Fe collection took place in the ballroom of a fancy New York City hotel. Nine hundred guests watched a parade of models strut down the runway to the sound of country music. As always, right in the front row sat Ricky, wearing a fringed shirt and a long prairie skirt. (Ralph's kids and Ralph's parents are usually there, too, as well as old friends—it's like a Ralph reunion, a big family affair!) The Santa Fe collection included many hits—coats and heavy cardigan sweaters inspired by the bold geometric designs on Navajo blankets; buckskin jackets; denim blouses with round, scalloped collars; and long, full skirts like the ones pioneer women wore.

It wasn't only the clothes that were so striking, but the jewelry and accessories that Ralph paired with them. He featured beaded earrings, heavy silver bracelets, and concho belts.

The Santa Fe collection changed the way stylish women dressed.

Behind the Scenes

At fashion shows, what the audience sees is very different from what's happening backstage. Behind the scenes, there's a lot of excitement. Makeup artists and hairstylists are rushing from model to model, fixing lipstick and smoothing hair; "dressers" check each model's outfit, sometimes retying a scarf, adjusting a hat, or changing a necklace. At the head of the lineup stands Ralph, who gives a final okay before a model can walk out. As with all fashion shows, the Santa

Fe collection represented months of work. So does Ralph get nervous? You bet! There are photos of Ralph backstage, peeking at the crowd, hoping people like what they see. The Santa Fe collection established Ralph Lauren as an international tastemaker. In the past, French designers like Dior and Chanel had set the style. Now, designers like Ralph created a style that was distinctly American. And he was not simply changing how women in the United States dressed; he was changing how women dressed all over the world.

CHAPTER 7
A Hard Year

Ralph Lauren was leading a charmed life. He kept opening more stores; he kept winning awards. He got to meet childhood heroes like Cary Grant and Frank Sinatra. Besides loving his work, he had a wonderful family. His parents had lived long enough to see his success and take pride in it. And Ralph was famous. In 1986, he was on the cover of *TIME* magazine. By now, Ralph Lauren has appeared on the cover of more magazines than any other designer in the world.

But the next year, 1987, marked the hardest time in his life. For a while, Ralph had been bothered by a strange ringing in his ears. When he went to his doctor to learn the cause of it, he received shocking news. He had a brain tumor, one that was growing quickly. Ralph had to have surgery to remove it.

The operation took five and a half hours, and afterward, Ralph spent several months at home recovering. Within the fashion industry, rumors flew that he was dying. That was not true at all.

Fortunately, the tumor was benign. That meant he didn't have cancer. Still, he had gone through a very difficult experience.

Time away from the office gave Ralph the opportunity to do a lot of thinking about what was most important in life.

One of Ralph's close friends was a well-known fashion writer and editor named Nina Hyde. Nina developed breast cancer, but she was not as lucky as Ralph. She died in 1990.

Looking for a meaningful way to honor his friend's memory, Ralph cofounded the Nina Hyde Center for Breast Cancer Research in Washington, DC, where Nina had lived and worked.

Nina Hyde

In the 1980s, the virus that causes AIDS was taking the lives of many in the fashion industry. Ralph wanted to help. So he donated a lot of money to help treat patients suffering from this terrible sickness.

Currently Ralph helps lead the fashion industry's effort to help women with breast cancer. The organization is called Fashion Targets Breast Cancer. Since 1994, it has raised millions of dollars to find a cure for the disease and to support women suffering from it.

Ralph also created Pink Pony T-shirts for women. Pink is the color associated with the cause for breast cancer awareness. So Ralph took his icon—the Polo pony—and turned it pink. Part of the money from sales of Pink Pony products goes to cancer research.

During his cancer scare, Ralph was fortunate to have the best medical care. But what about people who couldn't afford that? They deserved top-quality treatment, too. So he opened the Ralph Lauren Center for Cancer Care and Prevention in an underserved neighborhood in New York City.

Since then, it has treated thousands of patients. In England, he gave money for another cancer care center, the largest in all of Europe.

From childhood on, Ralph understood the power of books. They let children dream and encourage those dreams. So Ralph became partners with a New York publisher to promote literacy. (*Literacy* is the ability to read.) More than half a million books have been given to children who would not have been able to afford to buy them.

Coming from a family of immigrants, Ralph understood how special the United States was and how the country gave him the chance to follow his dreams. It was the reason he became involved in a special project. It was a way of showing his gratitude to the United States.

The symbol of our country is its flag, which Ralph has often put onto the design of sweaters and other clothes. His earliest memory of the flag was the one that flew from the flagpole at school, right across from his childhood home.

Probably the most famous flag in the nation is

the one that a composer named Francis Scott Key saw still flying after an important battle against the British in the War of 1812. He wrote a song about that flag, "The Star-Spangled Banner." The song became our national anthem.
The actual flag still exists but it was in terrible shape. That wasn't surprising since it was so old and cannons had been fired at it.

USA! USA!

Ralph Lauren has supported the United States in many ways. At the opening and closing of every Olympics, there is always a spectacular parade of athletes from every country. One after another, each nation's team marches around the main stadium, waving to the crowd. It is a moment of pride and celebration for the entire world. Since 2008, Ralph Lauren has had the honor of being the official outfitter of the US Olympic teams—both for the Winter Games in Vancouver and Sochi, and the Summer Games in Beijing, London, and Rio de Janeiro. The US uniforms for the Paralympic Games are also designed by—you guessed it—Ralph Lauren.

In 1998, President Bill Clinton and First Lady Hillary Clinton asked Ralph for his help restoring the flag. Ralph said yes right away and gave $13 million to do the job. It took eight years because every stitch in the flag had to be repaired. And the flag was enormous—thirty feet by thirty-four feet. Finally, in 2008, the original Star-Spangled Banner was put on display at the famous Smithsonian National Museum of American History in Washington, DC. You can see it there today.

CHAPTER 8
Into the Future

Thirty years after starting his company, Ralph Lauren was making many things besides clothes. He wanted his company to keep growing. In 1997, he decided the best way to do that was to go public.

Today, more than fifty years after the company's founding, it earns billions of dollars a year. In the beginning, Ralph made all the decisions. And he is still at work every day. But over time, he has hired executives to help lead different parts of his company.

Still, Ralph is the creative heart of the company. That is a big responsibility. At the end of a fashion show, after the models have left the runway, Ralph always comes out to take a bow. Often, he is in his favorite old work shirt and jeans. (He has always believed that clothes grow better with age.)

The crowd is clapping wildly. All cameras are trained on him. He sometimes tells himself, "Ralph, enjoy the moment." But usually, Ralph is thinking that tomorrow he has to start all over again, working on ideas for his next line of clothes. It never stops. He has to make everything new each season.

Going Public

Going public means people can buy shares in a company that used to be private. Buying a share is like owning a small piece of the company. If the company does well, the price of its shares will go up. A stockholder will make money. But if the company does

Ralph Lauren stock share

poorly, the stock price will go down. A stockholder loses money. Going public lets a company raise a lot of money, which can help it grow even bigger and more profitable. If you look in a newspaper on the financial pages, you can see what price the Ralph Lauren Corporation is currently selling for. It is represented on the New York Stock Exchange by the letters *RL*.

Ralph Lauren never thought of money as the most important thing in life. Yet he and his family enjoy the lives of the super-rich. There is a private jet to take the Laurens to their ranch, the Double RL Ranch, in Colorado; their house

on the island of Jamaica; their two-story Fifth
Avenue apartment; their weekend beach home in
Montauk, Long Island; and their country estate
in Westchester County in New York.

Instead of paintings, Ralph collects cars. For him, a great car is much more than something taking you from one place to another. It is an object of beauty. A work of art. Many of Ralph's cars are very valuable antiques. Some have been exhibited in museums. In his office, Ralph keeps miniatures of his favorites, including the newest electric Porsche, a Ferrari 250 GTO, and a very rare McLaren F1 LM.

But beyond the houses and cars and fame, Ralph Lauren has always held on to the values he was taught in childhood.

Long ago, from his parents, Ralph learned the importance of always giving your best and having faith in yourself, and as Ralph says, "being who you are." From his friends at school and at camp, he learned to be a leader. These lessons have stayed with Ralph all his life. He has had the good fortune of continuing to do what he loves and discovering talents in himself that he didn't know he had.

One sentence sums it up best. Ralph has said, "This is not a job. This is a joy."

The Lauren Family Today

Ricky has been married to Ralph for over fifty years. She is a psychologist and photographer.

Andrew, Ralph's oldest son, is head of Andrew Lauren Productions, which makes TV shows and movies. The offices are in New York City.

David has been working at the Ralph Lauren Corporation since 2000. He has helped with

advertising, launched the company on the Internet, and even once created a holographic fashion show! In 2011, he married Lauren Bush. They have a son, James.

Dylan, Ralph's only daughter, started her own business—but in candy, not fashion! The first of many Dylan's Candy Bars opened in 2001. She is married to Paul Arrouet and they have twins, Cooper and Kingsley.

Timeline of Ralph Lauren's Life

1939	Born on October 14
1957	Graduates from DeWitt Clinton High School in New York City
1964	Marries Ricky Low-Beer
1967	Launches Polo with wide neckties
1968	First line of men's clothes is launched
1969	Son Andrew is born, followed by David in 1971 and daughter, Dylan, in 1974
1971	First Ralph Lauren store opens in Beverly Hills, California
1972	The famous polo shirt with the Polo logo is introduced
1978	Clothes for children are introduced
1981	Receives his first award from the Council of Fashion Designers of America
1986	Flagship store in a restored mansion opens in New York City
	Appears on the cover of *TIME* magazine
1987	Recovers after surgery to remove a benign brain tumor
1997	Company goes public
1998	Donates money to restore the Star-Spangled Banner
2000	The Ralph Lauren Company becomes one of the first to sell on the Internet
2008	Becomes the official outfitter of the US Olympic teams
2017	Company celebrates its fiftieth anniversary

Timeline of the World

1939	Adolf Hitler's Nazi troops invade Poland, leading to World War II
1941	After Pearl Harbor in Hawaii is attacked, the United States joins World War II
1948	The modern nation of Israel is created
1955	Yankee Joe DiMaggio is inducted into the National Baseball Hall of Fame
1964	Beatlemania hits America The miniskirt becomes popular
1969	First moon landing occurs Woodstock rock music festival is held in upstate New York
1976	The United States of America celebrates its bicentennial
1979	John Wayne, star of many classic Western movies, dies
1981	Prince Charles marries Lady Diana Spencer
2001	Al Qaeda terrorists highjack four planes and attack the United States The iPod is unveiled
2006	Pluto is reclassified as a dwarf planet
2009	Barack Obama becomes the first African American president of the United States
2016	Hillary Clinton is the first woman to be a major political party's candidate for president
2017	*Vogue*, the fashion magazine for women, turns 125

Bibliography

* Books for young readers

Baird-Murray, Kathleen. *Vogue on Ralph Lauren*. London: Quadrille Publishing, 2013.

*Canadeo, Anne. *Ralph Lauren: Master of Fashion*. Ada, OK: Garrett Educational Corporation, 1991.

Lauren, Ralph and Mary Randolph Carter (editor). *Ralph Lauren*. New York: Rizzoli, 2011.

Lauren, Ricky. *The Hamptons: Food, Family and History*. Hoboken, NJ: John Wiley & Sons, 2012.

Trachtenberg, Jeffrey A. *Ralph Lauren: The Man Behind the Mystique*. Boston: Little, Brown & Company, 1988.